FORENSIC SECRETS

John Townsend

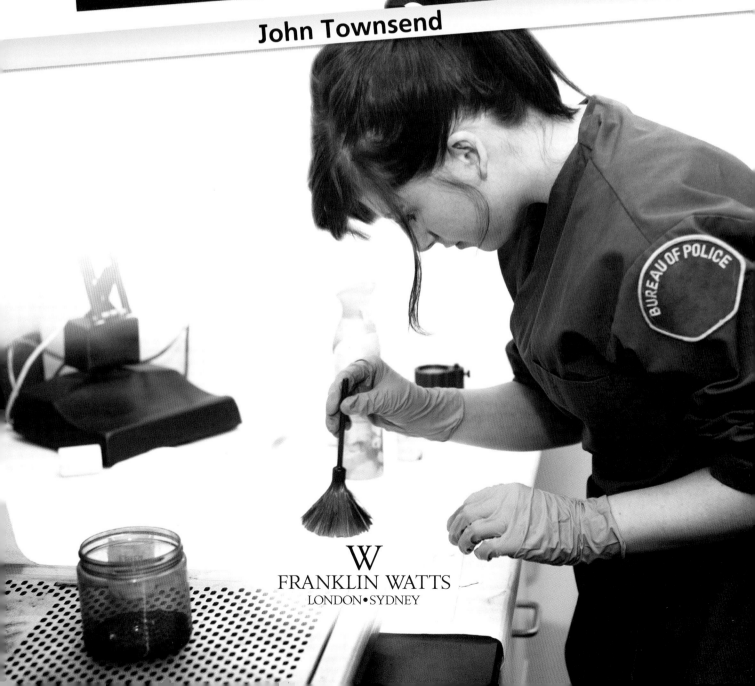

W

FRANKLIN WATTS
LONDON•SYDNEY

An Appleseed Editions book

First published in 2011 by Franklin Watts

Franklin Watts
338 Euston Road, London NW1 3BH

Franklin Watts Australia
Level 17/207 Kent St, Sydney, NSW 2000

© 2011 Appleseed Editions

Appleseed Editions Ltd
Well House, Friars Hill, Guestling, East Sussex TN35 4ET

Created by Q2AMedia
Editor: Katie Dicker
Art Director: Harleen Mehta
Designer: Cheena Yadav
Picture Researchers: Debabrata Sen, Nivisha Sinha

ISBN 978-1-4451-0384-6

Dewey classification: 363.2'5

All words in **bold** can be found in the Glossary on pages 30–31.

Website information is correct at the time of going to press. However, the publishers cannot
accept liability for any information or links found on third-party websites.

A CIP catalogue for this book is available from the British Library.

Picture credits
t= top, b= bottom, l= left, r= right
Cover images: Giorgio Fochesato/Istockphoto, Christopher Dodge/Shutterstock, James Ferrie/Istockphoto.

Peter Kim/Istockphoto: Title page, Stillfx/Shutterstock: Contents page, Corepics/Shutterstock: 4, Steger Volker/Photolibrary: 5,
German Ariel Berra/Shutterstock: 6l, United National Photographers/Rex Features: 6r, Peter Kim/Istockphoto: 7l, Steve Ross/
Istockphoto: 7r, Yuri Samsonov/Shutterstock: 8t, Grzegorz Kula/Istockphoto: 8b, Yuri Samsonov/Shutterstock: 9t, Nicole Weiss/
Istockphoto: 9b, Pool/Getty Images: 10bl, Rob Sylvan/Istockphoto: 10br, Charlie Schuck/Photolibrary: 11b, Jim Varney/Science
Photo Library: 12, Corepics/Istockphoto: 13, Andrew Chambers/Shutterstock: 14t, AFP: 14b, Jean Pierre Clatot/AFP: 15, BSIP/
Photolibrary: 16l, Corbis/Photolibrary: 16r, Dc Slim/Shutterstock, Vladm/Shutterstock, Ragnarock/Shutterstock: 17t, Sergey
Lukyanov/Shutterstock: 17b, Wolf Fahrenbach/Visuals Unlimited/Getty Images: 18, Pe Jo/Shutterstock, 19t, Charles Thatcher/
Stone/Getty Images: 19b, Bartomeu Amengual/Photolibrary: 20, Jonathan Parry/Istockphoto: 21t, Riekefoto/Dreamstime: 21b,
HelleM/Shutterstock: 22t, Frances Twitty/Istockphoto: 22b, Phil Walter/Getty Images: 23t, HelleM/Shutterstock: 23b, Candace
Schwadron/Shutterstock: 24, Photo Online/Shutterstock: 25t, Pokaz/Shutterstock: 25c, Pixtal Images/Photolibrary: 25b,
Keystone/Stringer/Getty Images: 26, Keystone/Hulton Archive/Getty Images: 27, CBS/Everett/Rex Features: 29, Frances Twitty/
Istockphoto: 31.

Q2AMedia Art Bank: 28.

Printed in Singapore

Franklin Watts is a division of Hachette Children's Books,
an Hachette Livre UK company.
www.hachettelivre.co.uk

CONTENTS

Tell-tale signs

Every criminal leaves clues behind, however careful he or she might be. Some clues are so tiny that it takes great skill for **CSI** teams to find **evidence** and work out exactly what happened.

Finding answers

A crime scene can be like a big puzzle. It may need **forensic** scientists to find and piece together every clue. Only then will the police know the answers to three big questions in any crime investigation:

- Who did it? (or who did not do it?)
- When did each part of the crime happen?
- How was the crime committed?

Every piece of evidence found at a murder scene is numbered, marked and photographed before it is taken away to the crime lab for closer study.

Hidden proof

Many criminals will try to hide all evidence that might link them to a crime. But they don't always know that forensic science can reveal some hidden secrets. Even if criminals scrub the whole scene spotless or destroy it with fire, forensic experts have clever ways of piecing together the 'invisible' clues of a crime puzzle. Every crime scene – a room, a car, a garden, a field or even a bombsite – can reveal a hidden story.

This book shows just how CSI scientists work to uncover secret, unseen or mysterious evidence – some of which you may be very surprised to discover…

SCIENCE SECRETS

In 1910, a French professor of forensic science, Edmond Locard, set up the first proper crime laboratory. He'd worked out that when two objects touch, they transfer **trace evidence**. Tiny particles such as specks of dust get moved from one thing to another.

Did you know that you leave tiny traces behind wherever you go? Experts use microscopes to study this trace evidence.

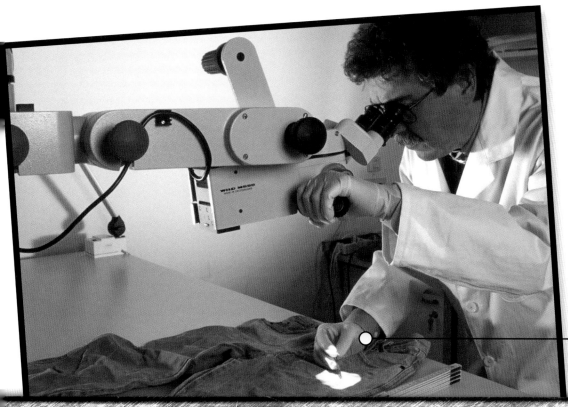

Some trace evidence is so small it is almost invisible to the naked eye. A microscope can help to examine clothing fibres.

Fingerprints

Every time you touch something with your bare fingers, you leave a smear of oily sweat behind. Your fingertips have a **unique** pattern of tiny ridges, which leave 'sweat prints' on whatever you touch.

Invisible clues

Using fingerprints to catch criminals is nothing new. In 1892, the British scientist Francis Galton wrote a book showing how fingerprint patterns could help to solve crimes. Ever since, the police have improved ways of finding fingerprints and matching them to **suspects**. Many criminals leave their unique prints at the scene of a crime.

Prints left as sweat marks, called **latent** prints, are often invisible. CSI teams now have ways to find and record these 'secret clues'.

Fingerprints glow under different lights, helping forensic scientists to see them clearly.

Fingerprint patterns are unique to every person.

Fine powder dusted over a surface will stick to the grease in fingerprints and make them visible. Sweat marks also glow under an **ultraviolet** (UV) light or a laser, so CSI teams now use special lights and goggles at many crime scenes.

Criminals try to avoid leaving fingerprints behind by wearing gloves or wiping clean anything they touch. However, forensic science is always developing ways to find and understand trace evidence – fingerprints can be just like a criminal's signature saying, 'I was here'.

These fingerprints could be the link to a criminal.

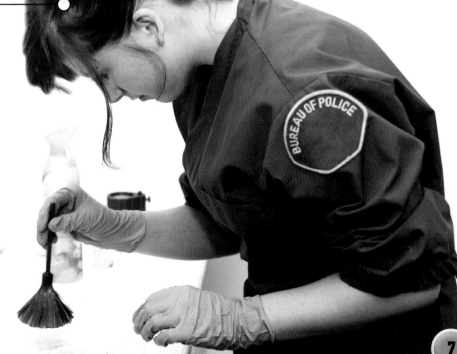

Forensic scientists use aluminium powder to reveal hidden fingerprints on items found at a crime scene.

Extra prints

If the ridge pattern of arches and loops on your fingertips is like no one else's in the whole world, what about the rest of your skin? Amazingly, your body has other hidden secrets, too.

Feet and toes

There are stories of **burglars** breaking into houses and taking off their shoes to creep around unheard. Although gloves may be protecting their fingers, a hole in a sock is enough to leave behind a toe or heel print. Just like fingers, bare toes, heels and the soles of the feet leave behind unique prints. A few criminals have been caught because their toe prints have given them away at a crime scene.

Footprints can be key evidence at a crime scene, but removing your shoes is no guarantee of secrecy.

CASE FILE

In 1952, a burglar broke into a bakery in Lanarkshire, Scotland. He used explosives to blow open a **safe**, which also blew flour over the crime scene. When the police arrived, they saw tracks across the floor and footprints on the safe. These were made by a bare foot, showing the ridges of a big toe.

A month later the police arrested William Gourley, a local criminal. They took his foot and toe prints and compared them with a photograph of the prints on the bakery safe. All measurements and details were identical. But would such evidence be allowed in **court**? The judge told the jury that this was the first time the police had tried to accuse a suspect on the evidence of a toe print alone. The jury had no doubt… GUILTY! Gourley was sent to prison for three years. His toe print had been his downfall.

DID YOU KNOW?

Your ears, tongue and lips can also leave unique prints behind. Tongue and lip prints are sometimes found at crime scenes – on drinking cups, cigarette ends or bottles. They can be used in investigations. So bank robbers beware – no drinking, licking or kissing at the crime scene!

The study of lip prints is called 'cheiloscopy'.

Invisible blood

A special chemical, called **luminol**, has helped to solve many murders. It has been the downfall of criminals who thought they'd hidden every scrap of evidence.

Unseen proof

A criminal will usually try to cover up all signs of a crime. If he kills someone, he'll need to get rid of the body and clean up the murder scene. That may mean scrubbing away all traces of blood. Then the police will have no idea a murder has happened at the scene. WRONG!

Before spraying luminol, the police see no sign of blood. After spraying it, they see the evidence they need: a bloodstained footprint.

DID YOU KNOW?

When luminol mixes with the iron in blood, it causes a chemical reaction, which makes it glow. Some types of glow-stick work in the same way. Shaking a glow-stick mixes two liquids (one is luminol), and wow... there is light!

In 1992, Chris Campano called the Oklahoma City police, USA, to report his wife Caren was missing. CSI officers called to look around the house, which was all clean and tidy. But when they sprayed luminol on a bedroom floor and shone a UV light, it lit up a large area of blood. This suggested someone had been hit with a blunt object and their blood was everywhere. Even if a room is scrubbed clean, traces of blood will remain. The police now knew this was a murder scene.

When they searched nearby wasteland, a year later, officers found a skeleton. The teeth matched Caren's dental records. Her skull had been smashed. Chris Campano was arrested and **convicted** of the murder of his wife. Luminol had helped to put another killer behind bars.

A tiny smear from a cut finger can leave a secret trace behind. Even after the victim is removed and the room cleaned up, forensic experts can find the tell-tale evidence.

Hidden clues

Drops of blood at a crime scene can reveal many secrets. Forensic experts can examine bloodstains to work out what happened and when. This is called blood pattern investigation (or blood spatter analysis).

Working out the story

Blood can drip, spray, ooze from a large wound, or fly off a weapon. At a crime scene, the CSI team will photograph the patterns of blood and interpret them. Blood may appear as a mixture of:

- Drops on a surface.
- Splashes, from blood flying through the air and hitting a surface at an angle.
- Pools or smears around the body, which suggest it has been dragged.
- Spurt lines from a major **artery** or **vein** in the body.

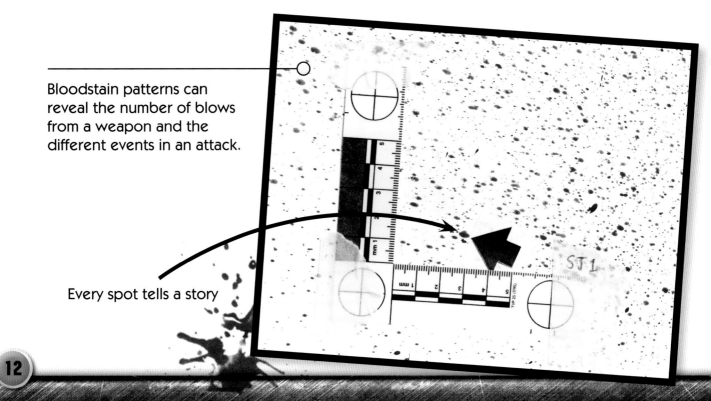

Bloodstain patterns can reveal the number of blows from a weapon and the different events in an attack.

Every spot tells a story

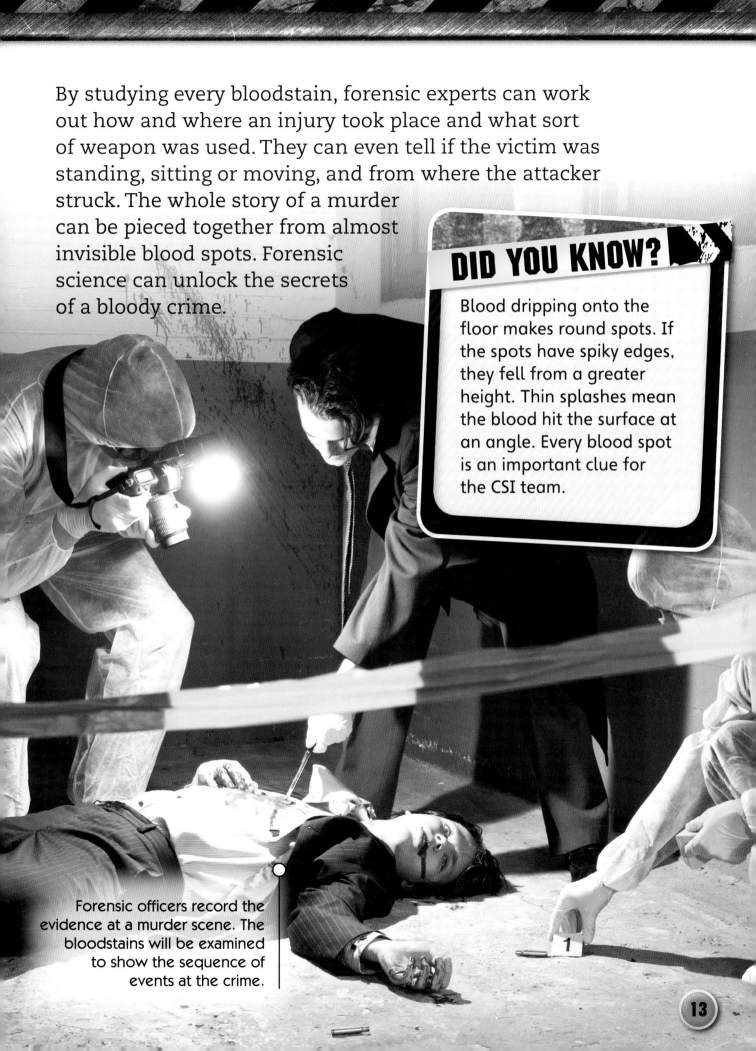

By studying every bloodstain, forensic experts can work out how and where an injury took place and what sort of weapon was used. They can even tell if the victim was standing, sitting or moving, and from where the attacker struck. The whole story of a murder can be pieced together from almost invisible blood spots. Forensic science can unlock the secrets of a bloody crime.

DID YOU KNOW?

Blood dripping onto the floor makes round spots. If the spots have spiky edges, they fell from a greater height. Thin splashes mean the blood hit the surface at an angle. Every blood spot is an important clue for the CSI team.

Forensic officers record the evidence at a murder scene. The bloodstains will be examined to show the sequence of events at the crime.

Secrets of a ski chalet

The case of a missing family of five in France made headline news in 2003. The family's disappearance was a real mystery – until a CSI team found tell-tale clues.

Missing link?

The Flactif family vanished without a trace from their chalet in the Alps, near the ski resort of La Clusaz. There was no sign of trouble at the empty chalet, where all the lights were left on, a fire was burning in the grate, the table was laid and dinner was in the oven.

The chalet's owner was Xavier Flactif, aged 41, who sold ski chalets to rich customers. His 4x4 vehicle had been parked on a nearby track, but a month later it was found far away. Something strange was going on. The chalet had been scrubbed clean and the children's bedding had gone, as well as a cut-out section of carpet. But there was no sign of a crime… until the police forensic team arrived.

Xavier and Graziella Flactif, with their children Sarah (11), Laetitia (10) and Gregory (7).

Grisly clues

Using luminol and laser lights, the CSI team found tiny flecks of blood between the floorboards. These were tested and shown to come from all five members of the family, as well as from one unknown person.

The big question was about the unknown blood. Tests eventually showed it matched a man renting the next-door chalet. As soon as he was arrested, David Hotyat confessed to killing the family after a terrible row over a small sum of money. The police later recovered the bodies in a nearby forest.

The scene of the crime near the popular ski resort of La Clusaz.

CAN YOU BELIEVE IT?

David Hotyat was found guilty of murder and sentenced to life in prison. His girlfriend was sentenced to ten years for her part in the murders. She denied killing anyone but said how much she hated the Flactifs. Without luminol, their terrible secret may never have been revealed.

GENDARMERIE

Proof on a pin-head

Everyone's blood is unique, just like a fingerprint. The tiniest speck of blood can tell scientists important information about the person it came from. It's enough to put a criminal behind bars!

Microscopic secrets

Even a tiny dot of blood on a pin-head is full of blood **cells**. Every single cell has material in it that can be examined with equipment in a laboratory. That's because every one of the billions of cells in your body contains a 'genetic code' – a set of 'instructions' that makes you who you are. This code is made of a substance called **DNA**.

Forensic scientists examine DNA databases to identify particular individuals.

These red blood cells have been magnified thousands of times.

It's not just blood at a crime scene that contains DNA – hair, skin cells (such as dandruff flakes), body tissue and body fluids (such as saliva and sweat) have DNA, too. Apart from some identical twins, we all have different DNA. Since the mid 1980s, forensic scientists have been able to compare DNA from cells found at a crime scene with a suspect's DNA, to prove if they were anywhere near the incident.

CASE FILE

In 2001, a 71-year-old woman was robbed in her home in Australia. The robber tied her to a chair and ran off with hundreds of dollars. As he ran, something fell off his body. It was a blood-filled leech, which CSI officers later found on the floor. Leeches drink blood, so CSI scientists had a perfect sample of the robber's DNA!

Years later, in 2009, a man was arrested for a drugs crime. The police took his DNA and it matched the profile on record taken from the leech. Peter Cannon pleaded guilty to the robbery he'd committed eight years earlier, and was sent to prison for the crime.

Australian leeches can vary in size from about 7 mm long to as much as 200 mm, especially when full of blood.

Sweaty secrets

Your body produces about a litre of sweat each day, to keep your skin damp and cool. During a crime, stressed criminals are likely to sweat a lot – which can help to catch them!

Sweaty work

CSI teams spend a lot of time at crime scenes looking for dried sweat on surfaces or on anything a criminal may have left behind. Just a few body cells are needed for forensic scientists to produce a DNA profile of the person they need to find.

This is what your fingertip looks like under a microscope. You can see fingerprint ridges and droplets of sweat.

DID YOU KNOW?

Although sweat itself does not contain DNA, it is usually full of dead skin cells that the body sheds all the time. These cells get left behind on clothes, glasses, masks and most things a criminal touches.

CASE FILE

When an armed robber held up a jeweller's shop in Norwich, UK, he didn't know a drop of his sweat would put him in prison. It was 2007 when Kulder Ojaaar from Estonia pressed a pretend pistol to a shop worker's throat. It left a smear of his sweat on her face just before he was chased from the scene. When the police arrived to investigate the crime, they took **swabs** from the shop assistant's face and collected traces of Ojaaar's sweat. Scientists got his DNA profile and checked it against known criminals around the world. Ojaaar was identified from Estonia's DNA database. It was just a matter of time before he was caught and put behind bars – which probably made him sweat even more!

CASE FILE

In 2008, a burglar broke into a house in Burbank, California, USA. When they arrived at the crime scene, 'police evidence technicians' found what they thought were traces of sweat on a window. They collected a sample and sent it to the Illinois State Police Crime Lab for DNA testing. The sweat was found to be an exact match to a known criminal, Stanley Francis, from Chicago. When Francis was arrested, he was carrying items thought to be stolen from other burglaries around Chicago. He'd been caught red-handed!

Computers can identify a suspect's DNA profile in seconds.

Sneaky saliva

Whether a criminal sneezes, froths at the mouth, dribbles with excitement or spits with rage, just a tiny drop of saliva left at a crime scene can be full of DNA evidence.

Throw-away DNA

Suspicious saliva full of DNA can be found in all kinds of places, such as:

- Where a mask or **balaclava** has been used as a disguise and left behind.
- Where a note is left with a licked stamp or envelope.
- Where cigarette ends, drinks bottles, apple cores, chewing gum or half-eaten food have been thrown from the window of a getaway car.

CAN YOU BELIEVE IT?

Some traffic wardens now carry a 'spit kit' to help catch angry motorists who spit at them. Wardens simply collect the saliva in the kit and send it to the lab for DNA testing. This has led to some foul-mouthed motorists being found and arrested for assault.

Chewing gum, coated in saliva, can be a rich source of DNA when left behind at a crime scene.

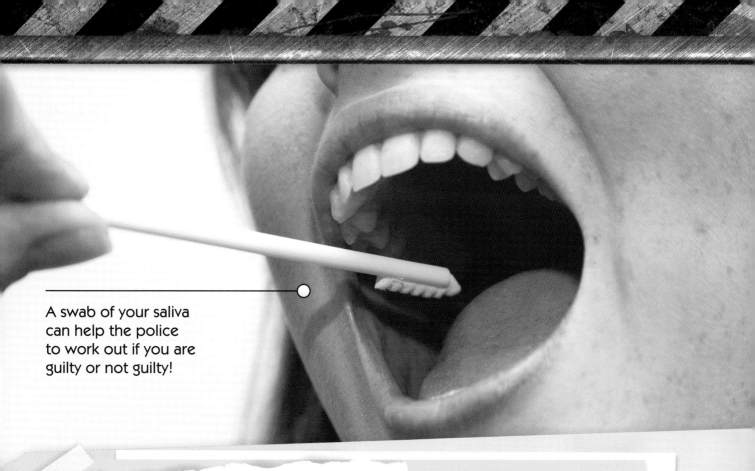

A swab of your saliva can help the police to work out if you are guilty or not guilty!

CASE FILE

The last anyone saw of 63-year-old Agneta Westlund of Sweden was when she took her dog for a walk in 2008. Her husband, Ingemar, went looking for her and was horrified to find her dead body near a lake. She had been attacked and killed. Ingemar called the police but they arrested him on suspicion of murder. He swore he hadn't killed his wife but he was the chief suspect – until forensic evidence proved he was totally innocent. Scientists found saliva and hair on his wife's body and they matched them to an elk!

An elk (or moose) is usually a shy animal but sometimes they eat rotting apples and become 'drunk' and violent. It seems one of these staggering wild beasts committed the murder.

Was this the killer?

Crash...

Most car crashes are caused by mistakes or mechanical failure. But what if a crash is really a crime scene and a cover-up for murder? Forensic scientists can find out...

Sifting through the wreckage

When the police investigate a serious car crash, they must work out how and why it happened. As well as examining the crash-scene, the road surface, skid marks and the position of the wreckage, the team will look for clues inside the vehicle. Photographs are taken from all angles. Forensic scientists then test the engine, instruments, brakes, tyres and the computer control system. Crumple zones of all car body parts can show precisely where different vehicles collided and at what speed.

The wreckage of a car holds many vital clues to the crash.

CASE FILE

In 1993, a police officer in Wales murdered his wife and faked a car crash to make her death look like an accident. Her **life insurance** would pay him well.

Steven Jones reported that his wife Madallin had died in 'a tragic accident'. He'd killed her with a blow from his truncheon, then put a bin-liner over her head to stop blood getting on his clothes. Wearing his police riot helmet to protect himself from injury in the staged crash, he drove his wife's body in her car to a lonely stretch of road and crashed into a tree.

Forensic tests at the scene later revealed her head injuries were 'inconsistent' with a road accident. The driver's seat was also set too far back for her to have been at the wheel. In the boot of Steven's own car, the police found his bloodstained helmet as well as a truncheon with traces of fresh blood on it. Sergeant Jones was sentenced to life in prison.

Forensic experts examine a burnt-out vehicle.

SCIENCE SECRETS

Forensic experts record blood patterns inside crashed cars to work out the chain of events from when the driver lost control to the actual point of impact. Blood evidence can also prove who was inside the vehicle and where they were sitting.

Fire

Even the blackened rubble and ashes left after a fire can hold clues for forensic detectives. Fierce flames, intense heat and smoke cannot destroy every bit of evidence.

Burning questions

Forensic experts will often be called to the smouldering remains of cars or buildings to work out if these were crime scenes. If the fire wasn't an accident, the crime of **arson** could have been committed.

Some criminals set fire to crime scenes to try to destroy the evidence.

DID YOU KNOW?

The USA Fire Administration reports that arson is the main cause of fires in the USA. Most often, fires are lit during the night, making it difficult for investigators to find a witness. The penalty for arson in some states is **capital punishment** if anyone was killed in the fire.

Arson investigators use many different techniques to find key information:

- The area of heaviest damage is likely to be the point where the fire started.
- Samples of burnt materials from where the fire started are tested for **flammable** substances such as petrol.
- The fire will be classed as either:
  1. natural, such as the result of lightning
  2. accidental
  3. deliberate
  4. unable to be identified
- Key witnesses are interviewed, such as fire-fighters, eyewitnesses, property owners, and neighbours.
- Is there a likely **motive** for the fire – would anyone benefit from it?

CASE FILE

In 2005, Thomas Sweatt was arrested for setting fire to more than 46 houses and apartments over two years around Washington D.C., USA. Two elderly women died in his fires. Fire forensic officers found Sweatt's trousers and hat at one fire scene. The crime lab matched the DNA profile from these items to Thomas Sweatt and DNA found at the other crime scenes. Sweatt pleaded guilty to all the fires, which he'd started to give himself a sense of power. He was sent to prison for life.

Even a burnt-out building can hold vital clues.

Explosion

Even in the wreckage after an explosion, forensic scientists can piece together shattered clues. Some criminals may think a bomb blast will destroy everything, including evidence. But they are wrong!

A huge jigsaw

When a bomb goes off, the explosive and its container shatter into tiny pieces and fly in all directions. The type of splinters and their position among the debris can give forensic experts vital clues about the bomb, maybe who made it, who planted it and where. Other wreckage and scattered pieces of the 'crime jigsaw' can give CSI experts key information.

Lord Mountbatten (third from left) was killed by a bomb blast on his fishing boat, four years after this photograph was taken.

CASE FILE

The terrorist bomb that killed Lord Louis Mountbatten (a relative of the British Queen) in 1979 was a famous case where forensic evidence from the crime scene convicted the killer.

Mountbatten's small fishing boat set sail from Mullaghmore harbour in Ireland, carrying seven passengers. Suddenly the boat was ripped apart by a bomb hidden on board, which killed four of the passengers (Lord Mountbatten, one of his twin 14-year-old grandsons, the boy's **paternal** grandmother, and a local boy Paul Maxwell, aged 15). When the forensic experts arrived, the crime scene was a mass of wreckage drifting on the water or spread across the seabed.

The police suspected an **IRA** man, Thomas McMahon, of planting the bomb. But what evidence could link him to the crime scene? The answer was green paint. McMahon's boot and anorak showed traces of four different types of paint, all of them matching the paint on Mountbatten's boat. The paint was also found on all four victims. This forensic evidence, including traces of explosives on McMahon's clothing, was enough to send him to prison for murder.

Lord Mountbatten, a cousin of the Queen, was 79 when he died.

SCIENCE SECRETS

Not all sand is the same. Grains of sand from various beaches look very different under a microscope. Sand grains on Thomas McMahon's boots were rounded and mixed with particles of sea shells. This mixture matched the beach sand where Mountbatten's boat was moored and was unlike any other sand nearby. It was more evidence to link McMahon to the crime scene.

What next?

New technology, the latest science and recent developments in forensic methods continue to improve CSI work all the time. Whatever will crime labs come up with next?

Future forensics

These are just some of the many ways in which amazing crime scene science is changing:

- New digital photography is developing ways to record specific evidence from crime scenes in a single photograph. The image can be used to measure distances and angles between objects precisely, as well as construct a 3D computer model of the crime scene.

- New methods can find invisible fingerprints and examine the chemicals in them. This process, called micro X-ray **fluorescence** (MXRF), zaps a fingerprint with a tiny X-ray beam that mixes with particles left behind from sweat. This can reveal the chemicals present in the fingerprint to create an image.

Sherlock Holmes (a character from old detective stories) used basic methods to catch criminals. CSI technology has come a long way since then!

- New handheld DNA testing machines will become part of a CSI team's equipment. These devices are an alternative to crime lab tests and can match DNA at a crime scene to a suspect in less than an hour. This means that the police can be faster on the tracks of a criminal on the run.

- New improved DNA techniques can test damaged samples which, until now, have been too poor to give results. Scientists can now take DNA samples from just a few cells left behind when a person has touched clothing.

Human rights?

Anything that improves the accuracy and speed of catching criminals is likely to make the world a safer place. But some people worry that new technology designed to 'catch crooks' could give the police too many ways of spying on ordinary people. These arguments are likely to become big topics in the years ahead.

CSI is a popular drama about forensic scientists. But not all crime scene investigations are as easy as television shows suggest!

CSI: CRIME SCENE INVESTIGATION

Glossary

arson
the illegal burning of a building or other property

artery
a blood vessel that carries blood from the heart to all parts of the body

balaclava
a woollen hood that some criminals wear over their head as a disguise

burglar
a criminal who breaks into someone's property to steal things

capital punishment
the death penalty for committing a crime

cells
the basic building blocks of all living things, continually being renewed

convicted
when someone is proven guilty of a crime in court

court
the place where a criminal is questioned and proven innocent or guilty

CSI
Crime Scene Investigation

DNA
the code in each person's cells that makes everyone unique

evidence
material presented to a court to prove the truth in a crime case

flammable
a substance that catches fire and burns easily

fluorescence
giving off radiation, usually as a glowing light

forensic
using scientific methods to investigate and establish facts in criminal courts

IRA
Irish Republican Army, a terrorist organisation in the 1970s

latent
present but not visible or obvious

life insurance
money paid to a named person when the insured person dies

luminol
a chemical to show up invisible blood spots

motive
whatever causes a person to do something or act

paternal
a relative on your father's side of the family

profile
a set of results often in the form of a graph that shows key characteristics

safe
a secure box where money or valuables are stored

suspect
someone thought to be guilty of a crime

swab
a cotton bud on a stick used for taking a sample of saliva or sweat

trace evidence
small amounts of material such as hair, pollen grains or soil that can be used as proof in a crime investigation

ultraviolet
light waves that shine deep purple and make some materials glow in the dark

unique
only one like it in the entire world

vein
a blood vessel that carries blood back to the heart from parts of the body

Index

Webfinder

www.abc.net.au/science/slab/forensic/default.htm
Find out more about the work of Crime Scene Investigators.

www.sciencenewsforkids.org/articles/20041215/Feature1.asp
Would you like to work as a forensic scientist? Find out more.

www.explainthatstuff.com/forensicscience.html
Find out how science can help to solve crimes, and try your own detective work at home.

www.crimescene-forensics.com
Learn more about some tried and tested forensic science techniques.

www.fbi.gov/fbikids.htm
This website from the FBI is full of games and activities to bring out the detective in you.